RUGBY

Contents

Published by Heinemann Library
an imprint of Heinemann Publishers (Oxford) Ltd
Halley Court, Jordan Hill, Oxford OX2 8EJ

OXFORD LONDON EDINBURGH MADRID ATHENS BOLOGNA
PARIS MELBOURNE SYDNEY AUCKLAND SINGAPORE TOKYO
IBADAN NAIROBI HARARE GABORONE PORTSMOUTH NH (USA)

© 1994 Heinemann Library

98 97 96 95 94
10 9 8 7 6 5 4 3 2 1

ISBN 0 431 07433 X

Designed by Ron Kamen, Green Door Design Ltd, Basingstoke, England

Illustrated by Barry Atkinson

British Library Cataloguing in Publication Data
Marshall, David
  Rugby. – (Successful Sports Series)
  I. Title II. Series
  796.333

Printed in China

Acknowledgements
The Publishers would like to thank the following for permission to
reproduce photographs:

Action-plus: pp. 20, 25, 29; Allsport: pp. 6, 8, 13, 15, 24; Colorsport:
pp. 3, 4, 7, 9, 11, 12, 21, 27, 28; Empics: pp. 5, 10; Meg Sullivan and
Andrew Waters: pp. 14, 16 (left, right), 17, 18, 19, 23; Andrew Varley:
imprint, pp. 1, 26.

Cover photograph © Colorsport

Thanks to Neil Tunnicliffe of the Rugby Football League's Public Affairs
Department for his comments.

The Publishers have made every effort to trace copyright holders.
However, if any material has been incorrectly acknowledged, we would
be pleased to correct this at the earliest opportunity.

Introduction

Most international sports cause great excitement but perhaps no other has quite the same effect on people as international Rugby. Rugby and all the excitement it generates are the result of a day in 1823, when someone who was playing football got carried away. The story is that one afternoon William Webb Ellis, a pupil at Rugby School, was playing in a game of football when he picked up the ball and ran towards the goal with it. This was clearly against the rules, but it was great fun, especially when the other team's players tried to catch him. A new game had been invented.

Many years passed before the game was properly organized. During the first few years it was common for matches to be played between teams of up to a hundred people, and on a pitch that was ten times bigger than today's.

In 1871 the first Rugby Football Union was created in England to organize the game. A number of clubs in northern England soon fell out with the Union's committee. The clubs thought that the best players should be paid for the time they took off work to play, and for the entertainment they provided for the people who went to watch them. The committee of the Rugby Football Union wanted their players to stay as **amateurs**. In 1895, 21 northern clubs broke away to form the Northern Football Union. This Union became the **Rugby Football League** in 1922.

Rugby is an exciting, action-packed sport.

Rugby League and Rugby Union 1

The two forms of the game, Rugby Union and Rugby League, have been poles apart since 1895, although both are now played in many countries in the world. The main object of each is the same: to score points by running with the ball and putting it down over the opponents' goal line, and by kicking the ball over the crossbar and between their posts. A game is played in two halves of 40 minutes each.

Rugby is played on a rectangular pitch and is always played on grass. In Rugby Union the pitch must be no longer than 100 m (109 yds) or wider than 69 m (75 yds). In Rugby League the pitch must not be wider than 68 m (74 yds).

The players in the teams

Rugby Union	Rugby League
15 players	**13 players**
8 forwards	6 forwards
7 backs –	7 backs –
1 scrum half	1 scrum half
1 outside half	1 outside half
2 centres	2 centres
2 wings	2 wings
1 full back	1 full back

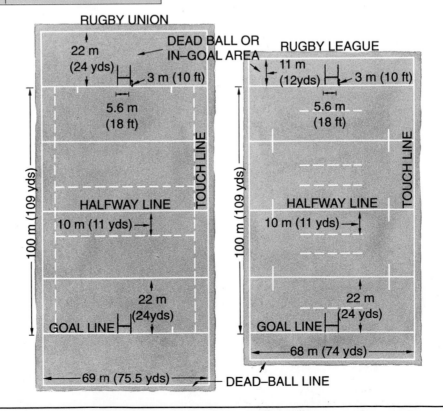

The Rugby League and Union pitches.

Behind each goal there is an in-goal area, or dead-ball area. In Rugby Union this must not be longer than 22 m (24 yds). In Rugby League this must not be longer than 11 m (12 yds). At the end of this area is the **dead-ball line**. At the centre of the **goal line** there are two posts 5.6 m apart (18 ft). The two posts are connected by a crossbar 3 m (10 ft) above the ground, making goalposts shaped like the letter 'H'. A line is drawn across the field 22 m (24 yds) from each goal line. In Rugby League, the game is sometimes restarted from behind this line.

Typical Rugby kit.

RUGBY FACTS

There is always a lot of running to do in Rugby, so any form of training will help you become a better player. There is a faster and more exhausting version of the game known as 'sevens', when only seven players take part. It is a useful way to get fit and to practise for the full game because all the players have to run, pass and tackle throughout a match.

Rugby Union is played with an inflated, oval ball which weighs between 400 and 440 grams (14 to 16 ounces). The ball is between 28 and 30 cm long (11 to 12 in) and between 58 and 62 cm (23 to 24 in) round the middle. The Rugby League ball is the same shape but slightly smaller.

The players' kit includes shirts, shorts, socks and studded boots. Although it is a very tough sport, protective clothing is not allowed in Rugby Union. In Rugby League players are encouraged to wear some form of shoulder padding. Most players wear gum shields to protect their teeth. Many of the forwards wear bandages round their heads, or special 'scrum caps', to protect their ears.

Rugby League and Rugby Union 2

R ugby League and Rugby Union may look the same at first, but they are really very different. Rugby League is a very open, fast game where the tackling is hard and seems to happen all the time. Rugby Union is slower because there are a lot more stoppages. Both games are exciting though, and easy to play if you are fit and strong and can think quickly. Both games are also simple, although the rules may seem complicated at first. It is important to be alert, and to think about the game at all times whichever version you are playing.

The use of the scrum is the most important difference between Rugby Union and Rugby League. On page 11 the **play-the-ball** movement in Rugby League is explained. This rule was introduced many years ago to keep the game moving. It meant that play did not have to stop for a scrum and meant the **forwards** were not being drawn into loose mauls and rucks.

In Rugby League the attacking team can keep the ball and play it back for no more than six tackles. After the sixth, possession goes to the other team in what is known as a **turn-over**.

Will Carling, in England kit, bursts through the USA defence.

Usually the team that has the ball on the sixth tackle will kick the ball as far forward as it can, to make sure that the other team takes possession a long way from their goal line. If they kick for **touch** they must make sure the ball bounces before it goes out (see page 7).

Both games are mostly played at amateur level, for fun. However, even at top levels, Rugby Union players are not paid for playing. This has caused a great deal of hardship for some Rugby Union players in the past. They either had to choose to give up some of their work in order to play, or they never had the time to practise and train properly. Some players changed to playing Rugby League professionally, where players are paid. In recent years many Rugby Union players have tried to introduce the rule that although they cannot be paid for playing, they can earn money from other things to do with the game. For instance, the England captain in 1993, Will Carling, was given permission to advertise Rugby kit, and be paid for it. If this rule on payment is gradually relaxed, then the style of play on the field will be the only major difference between the games.

Differences between Rugby Union and Rugby League

Rugby Union	Rugby League
Substitutes allowed only if a player is injured and cannot continue, or for blood injuries	Two substitutes allowed per game
Pitch 69 m (75 yds) wide	Pitch not wider than 68 m (74 yds)
In-goal area not longer than 22 m (24 yds)	In-goal area not longer than 11 m (12 yds)
Ball weighs 400–440 grams (14–16 ounces) and is 28–30 cm (11–12 in) long	Ball weighs 380–440 grams (13–16 ounces) and is 27–29 cm (10–11 in) long
Protective clothing is not allowed, except for mouthguards	Shoulder padding encouraged
Top players not paid	Top players paid
Tackling target is between the ribs and the knees	Tackling target is between the hips and the knees

Jonathan Davies of Warrington – a huge star of both Rugby Union and Rugby League.

Playing the game

The most important and obvious rule in Rugby, and the most irritating when you first start to play, is that when you pass the ball by hand it must be passed backwards or to the side. You can kick the ball forward, and you should always try to run forward, but the ball must not be passed forward. If you kick the ball forward you might find you are giving the ball to your opponents. It is often better to run and pass.

The kick off is always taken from the centre spot and is usually kicked so that the players in the team kicking off can run forward and get to the ball just as it is landing. At this point the battle for the ball begins. Players try to get the ball and pass it from hand to hand until it reaches their quickest runners – the centres and the wings. They will run towards their opponents' line. If they are tackled or stopped, they might lose possession of the ball. To avoid this they may kick the ball away from their own end of the pitch instead of running with it.

Rugby Union

The ball is often kicked out of play in Rugby Union. When it is kicked over the side-line it is said to have been kicked into touch. The side-lines are usually called the touch-lines.

In Rugby Union, when the ball goes out the game is restarted with a **line-out**.

A line-out.

RUGBY FACTS

In Rugby Union, if the players defending are between the 22 m (24 yd) line and their own goal line, they can kick directly for the touch-line and the ball can go out without bouncing in play first. If they kick the ball anywhere else on the pitch it must bounce first before going out. In Rugby League, all kicks from every part of the field must bounce into touch.

The USA and New Zealand Rugby Union sides lined up. Players are all different shapes and sizes in Rugby Union – but in Rugby League they are mostly the same size.

As shown in the picture, the two sets of forwards line up, side-by-side. The ball is then thrown between them by a player from the team which did not kick or carry the ball out. The tallest players in the team jump to catch the ball or to knock it back to their players behind them. The ball is then passed to the **backs** to start an attack. The front of the line-out must be at least 5 m (16 ft) in from the touch-line. There is a broken line on the ground from one end of the field to the other, and on both sides, to mark where line-outs should be started.

Rugby League

The line-out does not exist in Rugby League. Taking a line-out can be slow and so, many years ago in an attempt to keep the game moving more quickly, the organizers of Rugby League decided to use a scrum instead when the ball went out. With only six players in the scrum this was much quicker.

Scoring points

There are two ways of scoring points at Rugby – by scoring tries or goals. A try is scored by carrying or kicking the ball over the opponents' goal line and touching it down firmly before it reaches the dead-ball line. In Rugby Union a try is worth five points. In Rugby League it is worth four points. When a try has been scored, the scoring team can attempt a **conversion**. This means taking a **place kick**: the ball is put on the ground and aimed towards the posts. The kick must be taken in line with where the ball was put down behind the goal line, but at any distance back from the line. In order to be successful the conversion must pass over the crossbar and between the posts. A conversion is worth two extra points.

There are two other ways of scoring a goal. If a player kicks the ball on the half-volley (just as the ball touches the ground) it is known as a **drop kick**. If the ball goes over the bar and between the posts from a drop kick it is called a 'drop goal'. They can be attempted from anywhere in the field. Also, the referee can award a penalty kick for certain fouls. If the ball is then kicked between the posts – as in a conversion – points are scored. In both cases three points are scored in Rugby Union. In Rugby League a penalty kick is worth two points, and drop goals are worth just one point.

Sometimes a player breaks through the opponents' defence and is certain to score. The opposition may try to stop the attacker by committing a foul. On these occasions the referee awards a **penalty try** which, like a real try, is worth either four or five points depending on which game is being played. The conversion after this is taken from directly in front of the goalposts.

Neil Jenkins taking a place kick for Wales.

In Rugby Union, if the ball is kicked forward and goes over the goal line and one of the defending team touches it down before one of the attackers can, the game is restarted by a drop kick. This is taken by the defending team from their 22 m line. In Rugby League, you cannot touch down in your own in-goal area. You must either knock or carry the ball dead and restart with a drop kick from under your own posts, or you must carry the ball back into the field of play.

Rob Andrew taking a drop kick for England.

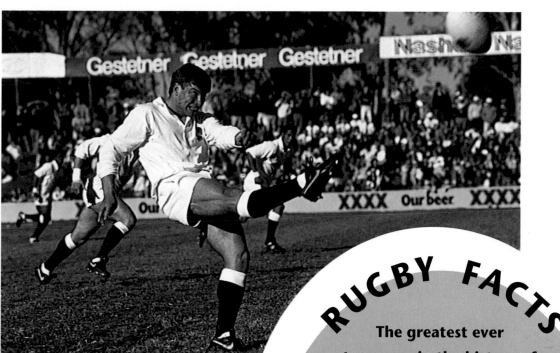

Point chart

	Rugby Union	Rugby League
Try	5 points	4 points
Conversion	2 points	2 points
Drop goal	3 points	1 point
Penalty kick	3 points	2 points
Penalty try	5 points	4 points

RUGBY FACTS

The greatest ever try scorer in the history of Rugby is the Australian, Brian Bevan. After docking at Portsmouth with the Australian Navy in 1945, he wrote to Leeds Rugby League club asking for a trial. They made the big mistake of turning him down and so he joined Warrington instead. In the next seventeen years, and two more with Blackpool, he scored 796 tries, over 200 more than the next highest scorer. By today's scoring system he would have scored 3184 points on his own – over 167 points a year.

The Forwards

I n Rugby Union there are eight forwards – in Rugby League there are only six. Their main job is to win possession of the ball and then to use it together with the backs. They are the members of the scrum. The scrum, or scrummage, is the way of getting play restarted by putting the ball into a set formation of the forwards. The first picture shows how a scrum is formed.

Rugby Union

Often when there is a foul in Rugby Union, the game is restarted with a **set scrum**. In Rugby Union the scrum is an important, and frequent event in a game. There are three players in the front row, two in the second row and three in the back row.

In Rugby Union there are rucks and mauls. A ruck is where a scrum forms when a player is going forward with the ball and is tackled, and the ball is on the ground. The rest of the forwards gather round and form the scrum. A maul is when players are moving forward in a group and the ball is being carried and passed at close quarters. Again, a sort of scrum set-up is formed. These sort of scrums happen in open or loose play as the ball is being passed, and are called **loose scrums**.

A Rugby Union scrum during a game between France and England.

The play-the-ball movement in Rugby League.

Rugby League

Scrums have three players in the front row, two in the second row and one in the back row. Scrums are not very important in Rugby League. Rucks and mauls do not happen. When a player is tackled he or she gets up and plays the ball back with a heel to a waiting team mate to pick it up and begin an attack. This is the play-the-ball movement. The picture (left) shows how the ball is played back. This play-the-ball does not happen in Rugby Union.

Scrums

The three players in the front row of the set scrum are the **hooker**, whose job it is to hook or heel the ball back when it is put into the scrum, and the **props**. All three are usually stocky and strong players. The props have to support the weight of the hooker as he or she tries to heel the ball back, and make a firm front line of the scrum for their team mates to push on. They try to overcome the opposing front row in the scrum in order to gain possession. In Rugby League, the props are often good kickers as well.

The second-row forwards, or locks, are usually the biggest players in the side. They have to use their strength in the scrums, and their height in the line-outs, to get possession of the ball. In England's successful Rugby Union men's team of 1991 the locks were over 2 m (6 ft 8 in and 6 ft 7 in) tall – and they both weighed over 100 kg (16 stone).

In Rugby Union, the back row is made up of two flankers – sometimes called the wing forwards – and a number '8'. In Rugby League, the back row is just one player, the number '13'. These players are known as the loose forwards because they are the first players to break away from the scrum and tackle the runners on the opposing team. They have to be quick as their job is both to help the player carrying the ball in an attack, as well as to be the first to a ruck or maul.

The play-makers

Rugby Union

The 'play-makers' are the scrum half and the outside half. Scrum halves are usually small, agile players. They act as the link between the forwards and the backs. From set scrums and loose play they must decide whether to pass, kick or run. They are often the noisiest players on the field, because they signal to everyone else what is happening.

Usually, the scrum half is able to make very long passes. Hours of practice are needed to be accurate. The first picture shows a diving pass, which lets the outside half who is waiting for the ball stand a long way from the scrum. This gives him or her more room to manoeuvre and time to think.

The outside half, also known as the fly-half or stand-off, is the pivot of the game. He or she controls most of the moves of the game since the scrum half will nearly always pass the ball straight to him or her from set pieces. An outside half must be able to pass well and be a good, tactical kicker.

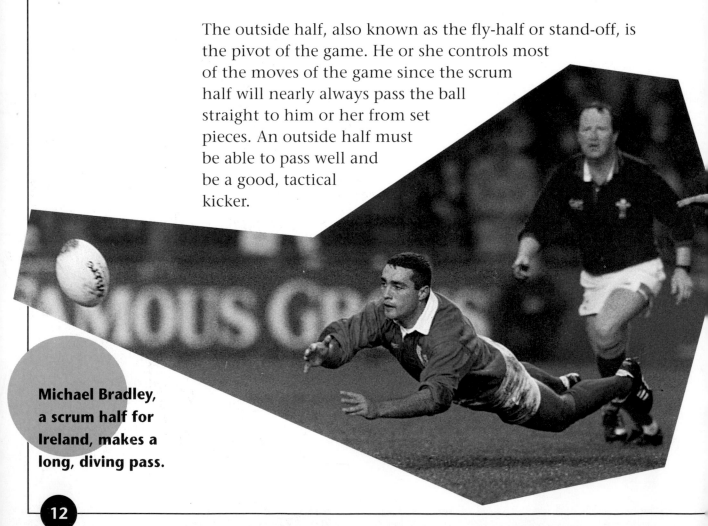

Michael Bradley, a scrum half for Ireland, makes a long, diving pass.

The scrum half and outside half must be able to kick well to touch – with either foot. Most great players kick equally well with their right and left feet. It is important that all players trying to play in these positions practise kicking quickly as well as a long way, with each foot.

An outside half must be able to judge the state of game in seconds and decide whether it is better to set the rest of the backs moving or kick instead. Because the outside half is in the middle of the field, he or she is the one most likely to be able to score by dropping a goal. This is a difficult skill on its own and needs a lot of practice.

Rugby League

There are three play-makers – the acting half back and two receivers. All three must be able to pass accurately over long and short distances and kick well. The acting half back is usually the hooker, but can be any player on the team. He or she stands behind the player who plays the ball and picks the ball up, then passes, kicks or runs.

Depending on the team's tactics, the acting half back can pass straight to a forward who will try to make ground close to the previous play-the-ball. Or they can pass further out to the first receiver, usually the scrum half, who can also pass, kick or run. If the team want to move the point of attack even further from the previous play-the-ball, they use a second receiver, usually the stand-off.

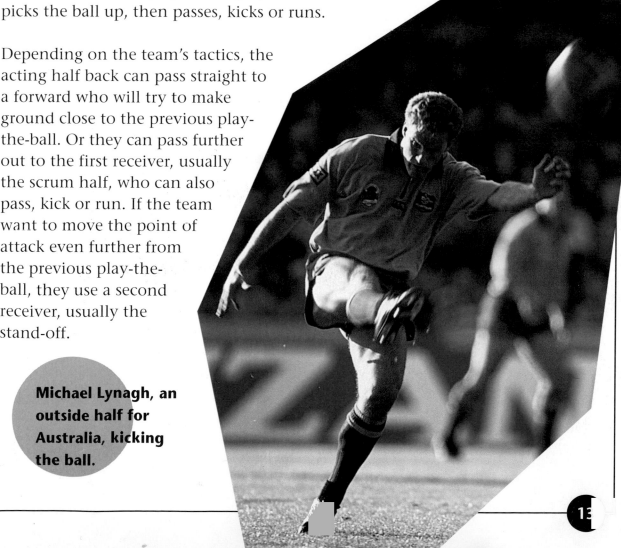

Michael Lynagh, an outside half for Australia, kicking the ball.

The dashers and defenders

To be a good centre or wing you must be a fast runner. Almost anything can be defended against except a lightning break from a centre or winger. Players have to be caught before they can be tackled, so if you do not like being tackled you must run as fast as you can!

When centres receive the ball from the outside half, they must run forward and either try to break through the opposition's defences or pass the ball on to their wings. In defence they must tackle well, and often. The centres should always run towards their opponents so that their opposite numbers are occupied. If a player is busy tackling, he or she cannot be attacking.

Like the centres, the wings should be fast runners. They should also have the skills to side-step, swerve and change pace. All these, but especially the side-step, should be practised. Try running forward and suddenly stepping to one side and running forward again. Try it slowly at first and then speed up. You should practise stepping first to one side and then to the other. The change of pace trick can be really effective too. Try running along and suddenly sprinting, and then slowing down, then sprinting, and so on.

How to stand to catch a high ball.

Frano Botica in action for Wigan.

RUGBY FACTS

Frano Botica, from New Zealand, is a Rugby League player who can play at scrum half, stand-off, centre, full back or wing. Wherever he plays he is always in the game, but it is his kicking that is rewriting the record books. In 1991 he became the fastest scorer of 1000 points in the game's history. Playing for Wigan against St Helens one day in 1992 he had ten chances to kick a goal – and kicked them all! He also scored a try on the same day, too.

The full back is the last line of defence. If you are a full back you must keep cool, even when under pressure. This is not easy when huge forwards are charging towards you at full speed. You must be able to catch the ball when it is kicked high in the air towards you and ignore any opposing players who might be rushing towards you. In Rugby Union, the full back is usually a good kicker both to touch and at goal. They are often the highest scorers in a match. As well as all these jobs the full back is expected to run forward and help the centres and wings to attack.

Attacking and passing

In the old days of Rugby Union, forwards concentrated on getting the ball. They were not expected to be able to run with the ball or tackle. This is not true today – all the players must be able to carry the ball and pass it to their team mates. The backs were not expected to be able to go in and take the ball away from their opponents, or tackle the opposing forwards. Today they have to be able to fetch and tackle, as well as run and pass.

To get your hands and arms in the right position, practise holding the ball and passing it without moving forwards.

A good, long pass should be just in front of the receiver.

Today, all Rugby players have to be able to pass the ball well if they are to attack successfully. The Rugby ball is easy to pass once you have the knack. To receive a pass well, you must keep your eye on the ball at all times. This is not easy when you have opposing players running towards you hoping to pull you down. You must look at where the ball is coming from and watch it until it is in your hands. You should 'reach for the ball' or push your hands towards the ball.

Once you have caught the ball you should swing your arms across your body and throw the ball towards the next player. The three pictures show how this should be done.

When you catch the ball you should take it in your hands. Because of the shape of the ball you should not try to catch it against your body. If you try to pull the ball into your body too soon, it could bounce away from you.

When passing the ball, hold it in front of you and look up to identify the player to whom you are passing.

The quicker you can pass, the better. If you pass the ball to the centres or the wings quickly they will have a better chance of getting through the opposition's line and going on to score. To be successful it is essential for a Rugby player to practise running and passing.

Pointers

Picking the ball up off the ground is one of the most difficult skills in Rugby, and it needs a lot of practice. Run alongside the ball and keep your eyes fixed on it. Bend down and scoop one hand underneath it, and put the other hand in front of it, to stop the ball being knocked-on. Keep calm and do not grab.

Defending

The only really successful way to defend is to make sure you are in the right place to tackle the player with the ball. If you tackle a player who has not got the ball you will give away a **penalty**.

The first aim of the tackle is to stop the person in front of you. The second aim is to try to stop the ball from being passed as you tackle your opponent. The first is fairly easy to accomplish and should be practised so that as little harm as possible is caused by the tackle.

Sumo wrestlers crouch low and then drive forwards and upwards to overcome their opponents. A Rugby tackle should be attempted in the same way. There are hard bits on the human body that can hurt. When driving into a tackle you should avoid them as much as possible. The ideal target area is between the ribs and the knees in Rugby Union. In Rugby League it is between the hips and the knees. If you try to grab your opponent above the shoulder you will be guilty of high tackling and will give away a penalty.

When your opposite number runs towards you, you must wait until they are within tackling range.

Safety first

If your tackle is lower than the knees, you will be in danger of catching a boot in your face.

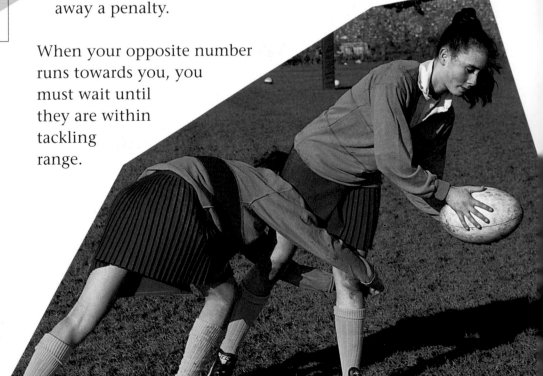

A good tackle.

Tackling a player
without the ball is
forbidden. Tackles
around the head and
neck are both
dangerous and
against the rules.

Do not commit yourself too soon; they may just side-step and leave you clasping thin air. You should drive your shoulder into their thigh and wrap one arm around the front of their legs. The other arm should then come round the back of the legs. The result is that your opposite number cannot move forward without falling over. It is especially important to remember where to put your head when you are tackling. Always put it behind the player you are tackling, not in front. If your head is in front, the other player's legs may fall on you as they go down.

There are many ways of practising the tackle. One way is to go through the whole sequence described above at walking pace. Then you gradually speed up until you are tackling in the way you would in a game.

There is a lot of satisfaction in making a good tackle. It is a good idea to keep a count of your tackles in a game to know how well you are playing. Try to beat your own total in every game you play. You know that every time you make a tackle you have successfully defended your own line.

Practising
tackles on a
tackle bag.

Fouls and penalties

Players can break the rules in a number of ways, usually by trying to take an unfair advantage over their opponents. If the foul is a serious one that could be dangerous, or deliberately stops the play, the referee will give a penalty or send the player off the field. A penalty can be kicked over the posts for two or three points (see pages 8 and 9). If the foul is not serious, the referee will award a free kick which cannot be kicked for a goal.

Rugby involves handling an awkwardly-shaped ball. This means that quite often players will knock the ball forward with their hands when they are trying to catch it. If they do, it is called a **knock-on** and a scrum is awarded, with the ball given to the side that did not foul. Because of the way the forwards go down into the scrum, the ball will get to the hooker first who is on the side putting the ball in. So their team should always get possession from the scrum and be able to start an attack.

The scrum half putting the ball into the scrum.

Sometimes, to gain an advantage, the hooker will try to hook the ball back before it is actually in the scrum. This is known as foot-up and will be punished by giving away a free kick to the opposing team.

Rugby Union

One of the most dangerous fouls that forwards can commit is to collapse the scrum deliberately. Instead of trying to stay upright and push for the ball, the forwards would pull the scrum down on purpose. This is dangerous because of the pressure on the necks of the players at the front of the scrum.

Although the players in a line-out are usually tall, they sometimes try to get even higher to reach the ball, by leaning on the shoulders of their opponents, or by being lifted by their team mates. Both these actions are against the rules and will lead to a penalty. The jumpers in the line-out are easily pushed away when they are jumping from the ground. Any player who deliberately pushes or barges an opponent in the line-out will give away a penalty.

Rugby League

When a player has made a tackle, they must get off the tackled player straight away, and allow them to play-the-ball. When a player is playing the ball, the defending player marking them cannot push or kick them. If either of these rules are broken a penalty is given away.

More fouls

The **offside** rule in Rugby sounds very easy, but can be difficult to understand when the game is being played. Players are offside when they are in front of the ball and attempt to play it, or get in the way, after it has been played by a team mate. This means that after a player has passed the ball, he or she should drop back behind the player the ball has been passed to. If a player kicks the ball up the field it is a good idea for them to chase after it so that all the players on the same team are behind him when the ball is caught. At the scrums and the line-outs there are more complicated offside rules.

The positions of players when the ball is kicked forward, showing how many players would be offside if they played the ball.

After catching a kick, or a long pass, a player running forward can sometimes come into contact with one of their team mates. This would make the team mate offside. However, providing he or she does not get involved in the game, and is not standing in the way, the offside rule does not apply.

Rugby League

When the play-the-ball movement is taking place, the defending side must be 10 m (11 yds) behind the players playing the ball, except for the two players marking them. The attacking side must be 5 m (5.5 yds) behind. Otherwise, the players are offside.

OFFSIDE FROM A SCRUM

Players 1 to 3 have advanced too far and are offside.

The ball

1 2 3

Team A
Team B

HALFWAY LINE

Another way a player can be offside is when the ball is on the ground and several players are trying to get it back to their team. If they go too far forward they will go over the ball and be offside. This is known as 'going over the top' and is one of the commonest fouls of all. Because of the play-the-ball movement this never happens in Rugby League. Some players will do this deliberately in order to stop the other side from getting the ball, but more often it happens accidentally. It is always punished by the award of a penalty.

A player lying on the ball and being offside – 'over the top'.

In Rugby Union, when players are tackled, they must always let go of the ball and not touch it again until they are back on their feet. If tackled and on the ground, a player must not pass the ball to a team mate. In Rugby League, players keep hold of the ball.

Famous players

Two of the most famous English Rugby Union players are a winger born in Russia and a lock who was forced to retire when he was looking forward to at least five more years at the top. The Russian, Prince Alexander Obolensky, was born in St Petersburg and came to England when his family lost their home in the Russian Revolution in 1917. He played four times for England and scored a famous try against New Zealand in 1936. Bill Beaumont was the lock and was the captain of the very successful England team of 1980, winners of the Grand Slam. He also captained the British Lions in 1980. He received a bad head injury during the 1982 County Championship Final and doctors told him he must never play again.

Serge Blanco of France in action.

Serge Blanco is the most-capped player in the Rugby Union Five Nations championship. He played 93 times for France. The second most capped player is Phillippe Sella, also of France. Mike Gibson, of Ireland, played 81 times for his country. He also played twelve times in total for the British Lions, which puts him level with Blanco.

The most famous Rugby Union try ever scored on TV was probably by the Welsh scrum half, Gareth Edwards. He was playing for the **Barbarians** against the touring All Blacks when he joined in a passing movement that started on their own line and finished with him scoring at the other end.

Jim Sullivan played Rugby Union for his home town of Cardiff before turning professional in 1921. He joined Wigan to play Rugby League and stayed with them for 32 years. First he was a player, and then a coach. During his career as player he kicked an incredible record 2867 goals.

Va'aiga Tuigamala, the All Black try-scorer who joined Wigan to play Rugby League in 1994.

Va'aiga Tuigamala signed for Wigan at the end of the 1993 New Zealand All Blacks tour of Great Britain, but didn't play until February 1994. He had to get fitter to be able to play Rugby League – as well as running with the ball, League players make up to 50 tackles in a match. He is now a stone heavier – and it's all muscle!

Clive Sullivan, a Welshman who played as a winger for both Hull and Hull KR between 1961 and 1985, was the first black player to captain a Great Britain side in any sport when he took charge against France in 1972. He played in seventeen Tests between 1967 and 1973, and was captain in nine of them, scoring thirteen tries. He was awarded the MBE in 1974.

Cups and leagues

Rugby Union

England, Scotland, Wales, Ireland and France are the five countries who play every winter in the international tournament known as the Five Nations. If a country manages to win their four matches then they are said to have achieved 'The Grand Slam'. Each country plays two games at home, and two away. The four 'home' countries without France play for an imaginary trophy called the Triple Crown.

The World Cup in Rugby Union takes place every four years. The two greatest Rugby Union nations in recent years have been the Australian Wallabies and the New Zealand All Blacks. The South African team was always one of the greatest in the world. Until recently they were banned from international Rugby for political reasons. More and more African nations are developing their Union sides. Namibia, Zimbabwe and Kenya will be trying hard to do well in the next World Cup.

The Women's Rugby League 1991 Cup match.

Even though the women's game only started 20 years ago, there are now hundreds of Women's Rugby Union clubs all over the world. In Britain there are more than 250 clubs and around 10,000 women play regularly. The first women's World Cup was held in 1991 and won by the USA. They beat England 19–6 in a final held at the famous Cardiff Arms Park. The 1994 competition has twelve countries taking part, including the five nations, Russia, Spain, Canada, Kazakhstan, USA, Sweden and Japan.

RUGBY FACTS

In Rugby Union, every three years a team selected from the four 'home' countries tours different parts of the Rugby-playing world. This team is known as the British Lions. In Rugby League, the British side is always made up of players from the 'home' countries and called the Lions.

The New Zealand All Blacks performing their 'war dance' – the Haka – before a game.

Rugby Union used to be one of the Olympic sports. Rugby featured in just four Olympics. In 1900 France were the winners. In 1908 Australia beat Britain to win the gold. In 1920 and 1924 the USA beat France. Daniel Carroll in the USA team won his second Olympic gold in 1924 – his first had been for Australia in 1908.

Rugby League

There are five full members of the International Board: Great Britain, Australia, New Zealand, Papua New Guinea and France. Great Britain and Australia play each other for the Ashes every two years.

There are also amateur organizations in Russia, South Africa, Morocco, Fiji, Western Samoa, Tonga, Japan, USA and Canada. They enter sides in the World Sevens tournament every year. Some of these countries, together with the five international teams, will qualify for the Centenary World Cup in Great Britain in 1995. Rugby League has a World Cup tournament every four years.

There are nineteen clubs in the Women's Amateur Rugby League Association, each of which have teams at various age levels. Girls play along with boys at junior level.

Rugby highlights

On Fiji's Rugby Union tour of Argentina in 1980, their outside-half, Senegakali, kicked the ball so far out of touch that it went out of the ground. Despite all their searches they could not find it. The only other ball was so flat and old that neither side thought it was suitable for play. The game had to be abandoned with Fiji winning 24–9.

You do not need many players to have a successful international side. The state of Andorra has just one club with around 50 players, and they became champions of the Spanish League in 1976. This is the only occasion when a country has won a club league championship.

You do not have to start playing Rugby when you are very young. The greatest try scorer in International Rugby Union is David Campese of Australia. He scored his fiftieth try in internationals in 1992. He did not play the game at all until he was seventeen. By the time he was nineteen he was playing for Australia.

David Campese outrunning the Argentinian defence.

The Caribbean Sea is the backdrop to this game in the Jamaican sunshine.

Rugby Union started in Barbados by accident in 1933. Trinidad's rivals in British Guyana had run out of money and could not afford to host them. They suggested that Barbados might like entertain them instead. The Barbadians protested that they had no pitches, no teams, no kit and no facilities. Trinidad told them that all they had to do was 'put fifteen reasonably fit young men on a field.' The first Barbadian side was created.

Francis Cummins of Leeds broke the record for youngest player in a Rugby League Challenge Cup final in April 1994 at 17 years 200 days. Paul Newlove holds the record for youngest player for Great Britain at the age of 18 years 72 days, against New Zealand in 1989.

Until recently, white settlers in Africa generally dominated Rugby Union. Things are changing quickly throughout Africa, with teams solving racial problems and tackling shortages of equipment and facilities in some countries. However, the South African side has only ever fielded three black players. In contrast, after independence Kenya became an all black side overnight, and only allowed whites to play again in 1993.

Glossary

amateurs People who play the game for fun, not professionally.

backs The attacking players, not in the scrum, sometimes called the three-quarters.

Barbarians A Rugby Union team which plays occasional special matches, selected from the best players from all over the world.

conversion A successful kick over the crossbar and between the posts after a try has been scored.

dead-ball line The last line across the field behind each goal. If the ball crosses this line then the game has to be restarted on the field.

drop kick The ball is dropped from a player's hands and kicked as it touches the ground.

forwards The players who make up the scrum and win the ball for their team.

goal line The line across the field that passes through the goal posts, over which a try can be scored.

hooker The forward in the middle of the front row of the scrum who hooks the ball back with his foot.

knock-on The ball is knocked forwards, towards the opposing goal line, with either the hand or the arm, and touches the ground or another player.

line-out The two teams in parallel lines facing the touch-line when the ball is thrown between them to restart the game after it has been put into touch.

loose scrum A scrum formed in open play when two or more forwards gather round to get the ball back to their own team.

offside If you are ahead of a team mate who has the ball, or has kicked the ball, you are offside.

penalty A kick given to the non-offending side when a foul has been committed.

penalty try A try awarded when the defending team commits a foul that prevents a certain score by the attackers.

place kick A kick made after placing the ball on the ground. The usual kick for converting a try.

play-the-ball In Rugby League, a tackled player gets up and plays the ball back with a heel to a team mate, who picks it up and begins an attack.

props The two players on each side of the hooker on the front row of the scrum.

set scrum When the forwards in each team link together after a foul and to restart the game.

touch If the ball contacts, or goes over, the line at the sides of the field it is 'in touch'.

turn-over In Rugby League when after six tackles possession of the ball is given to the other team to attack with.

Index